To Lou,

Thanks for the

laughs!

Lee Vogel

Huffin' 'n Puffin': Living With COPD

Leland Gordon Vogel

Copyright © 2004 by Leland Gordon Vogel

ISBN 0-7414-2227-1

Published by:

INFI∞ITY
PUBLISHING.COM

1094 New DeHaven Street, Suite 100
West Conshohocken, PA 19428-2713
Info@buybooksontheweb.com
www.buybooksontheweb.com
Toll-free (877) BUY BOOK
Local Phone (610) 941-9999
Fax (610) 941-9959

Printed in the United States of America

Printed on Recycled Paper

Published December 2004

Dedications

To COPD Patients

I dedicate this book to every patient with a life-threatening ailment, past, present and future – but, especially COPD patients. Contrary to some opinions, most COPD patients did not invite life-threatening chaos into their lives. However, once afflicted, these people fight through their fears, turmoil and ailments to demonstrate the most awesome courage and strength imaginable. To meet and witness each of them is an inspiration.

To Sandy Carter

This book has become reality because of her encouragement and support. Friend, caregiver and significant other in my life – well, I owe her a lot!

Acknowledgements

My Thanks

The Veterans Administration

In the past few years the VA has taken some hard knocks about the care delivered to veterans. In my case, I feel the world needs to know that the health care delivered to me has been excellent. Except for delays caused by volumes of people in the system, the Seattle VA Healthcare System (including the University of Washington Physicians) delivered on their promises, made me better and have continued with my follow-up care.

When discussed with other patients in the recovery room, the consensus of opinion was the same. Each of my roommates were pleased with their care and felt that the VA had delivered on their promises to us. For those patients and myself, thank you.

Friends and Family

I also want to thank all the people who encouraged me to pursue my writing and complete this book. Without your encouragement, this book would not likely have been developed. Thank you.

The Cover Art

"Turmoil and Promise" © 2000 Leland G. Vogel

The world of a COPD patient is shrouded in turmoil, our path like walking on water as we reach for every ray of hope – each new dawn a precious gift.

While I have many pictures of this lake view, this picture best exemplifies the feelings of COPD patients.

Huffin' 'n Puffin':

Living With COPD

Prologue

This story chronicles events that took place from September 1997 through July 2004. Like most patients with a serious ailment, I have since learned that I probably contracted my ailment much earlier. In my case, that would have been in May 1993. Although I visited general practitioners at that time for an unusual abdominal problem, they were unable to diagnose an ailment of any kind.

Welcome to my world. Like so many millions of people, my world includes a disease called COPD – Chronic Obstructive Pulmonary Disease.

COPD is a catchall phrase that includes most lung diseases and breathing disorders. These diseases afflict 13 million people. COPD is the 4th largest killer disease and the 3rd largest reason for disability. Disease definitions include chronic bronchitis, emphysema, asthma, black lung disease, as well as many, many others. It does not matter what the baseline cause of someone's disorder may be, the impact on the body is much the same for everyone – debilitating due to lack of oxygen in your blood stream. The lung/s have become ineffective at helping to distribute oxygen the body needs to properly function.

When we first learn we have these disorders, the knowledge itself can be overwhelming! Depending upon whether the disease was detected early or late in its development may determine the degree of debilitation a patient will experience. No two patients are the same. Complicating external factors may be dust, pollen from weeds, trees, grass or flowers, plus dirty air, smoke from tobacco products, trains, trucks, smog, fireplace smoke, business pollutants, auto pollutants, possibly perfumes or fragrances and numerous other things we encounter in our daily lives. Internal complications can be any other malady you may have, including the common cold, flu or allergies. Each of these, and more, are triggers that can occur at any given moment of any day or night, regardless of where we are or what we are doing. That volatility creates its own chaos in the life of a COPD patient and for their loved ones. It will cause many plans to be altered or cancelled.

The medical community continues to get better at treatment and diagnosis. For some of us the affliction can be a death sentence, but that does not need to be true today. Operations like LVRS (as in my own case) are 'quality of life' efforts – to extend and make your remaining time on Earth comfortable and livable. Many people live 25-35-45 years after contracting COPD.

Newly diagnosed COPD patients have no idea what to expect, what the terminology is, what kinds of tests or treatment will follow, what is expected of us or anything else. We are suddenly catapulted into a foreign world – a scary world, regardless of our age or background. Add to that the daily trauma we experience while suffering with the disease and you have a very volatile mixture that can lead to all manner of behavior, depression and grieving.

The reason for this book is to share the practical knowledge gained from my experiences with COPD. Newly diagnosed COPD patients have much to learn and experience. Hopefully, these pages will shed light and a small bit of levity on areas of concern and frustration for you or a loved one. If my words influence or stop someone from smoking or help anyone with COPD, my efforts will be an overwhelming success!

I am no medical professional, just a pioneering computer 'techie' who has been forced to learn more than he really wanted to know about the body because of emphysema based COPD. Hopefully my experiences will simplify a learning curve or give practical insight to one possible future, as well as what might be experienced along the way.

I have chosen to write in the form of poetry – organized chronologically from the moment I learned that I had contracted the ailment. This method allows me to relate a story line that you can easily follow all the way through my rehabilitation.

As a devotee of double-entendre, I chose the name Huffin' 'n Puffin' because it has double meaning for COPD patients. First and foremost the meaning is for the way we patients breathe and survive every day – shallow huffs and puffs, often labored. Secondly, the meaning has to do with how we breathe while and after exercising - a daily ritual following rehabilitation. Together, they reflect how we live with COPD.

When you are diagnosed with an ailment like Chronic Obstructive Pulmonary Disease (COPD), it *will* change your life and your perspective on everything! You do not understand why things are happening the way they are; suddenly, you simply are forced to realize that life has changed. You now have to learn to deal with life from a totally new perspective. It is a huge adjustment! The changes are enormous!

No two days are alike! You will experience something new and different every day for the remainder of your life. Get used to it! You have joined 'life in the slow lane'.

Changing Perspectives - III

Life had been good, been riding the wave,
Had a great family, even had a nice cave.
Managed to reach fifty, plus five with a rave,
Kids were all grown, no thought of a grave.

When all of a sudden, one day came a pain,
Could not explain it, didn't come with the rain.
Went to see doctors, they all tried in vain,
To diagnose ailments, even tried the veins main.

Many months later, a diagnosis grew clear,
A breathing disorder, emphysema - no cheer.
Then finally COPD was declared in full gear,
It's really shocking; it'll fill you with fear!

For when you get sick, all things you hold dear
Are suddenly changed, just breathing's hard here!
I medicate daily, taking great care just to steer,
A course back to wellness, no time for a tear.

Now singing and playing the music I adore,
Often laughing, loving or just yelling 'fore!'
Must wait for doctors who can tell me once more,
"Resume your great life, we suggest with amore!"

Now I sit waiting for the doctors to save,
What's left of my lungs, so I won't be a slave
To the simplest of chores, trying just to behave.
I'm here to tell you, it can hurt just to shave!

In spite of the ailment, the future looks bright,
Enjoy every moment, every smell and delight.
Our life is a treasure; it's worth the good fight,
Overcome your frights, the results will be right!

For most COPD patients, the early signs or symptoms of trouble are so minute, so insignificant that they are 'undetectable'. They seem to 'just happen'.

I have since learned that most of these instances are rooted in denial that we are getting ill. Men are the worst at denying things like this, always feeling like we are 'super human' or in some way just cannot be brought down. WRONG! I admit it. I was among these men. Except for a common cold or an infrequent flu bug, I was never sick one day in my 60-year life. I always realized my good fortune and thanked the good Lord for my health every day.

For most of us who have a developing health problem, there is a moment in time that clearly identifies when a health problem has materialized and you had better deal with whatever that problem is – and quickly!

The First Signs

I'd cleaned my apartment, all day for a guest,
Who was going to visit, staying at my request.
It had been a long time, the dust billowed I jest,
Had I realized the scare, I'd have hired the best!

Two days I had labored, breathing dust as I went,
Bouncing with energy, opening windows to vent.
Washing windows and floors, I'd made a good dent,
When my guest arrived, I behaved like a gent.

We had a great visit, took in a show,
Stopped for a beer, watched the moon glow.
Retired for the night, I suddenly woke with a woe,
Gasping for air and was feeling real low!

Stumbling to phone, I nearly called nine-one-one,
While gasping, struggling, this was no fun!
Reaching the phone, I suddenly realized don't run,
I'm hyperventilating! Breathe deep 'til I'm done!

I sat on the couch for the rest of the night,
Coughing, wheezing, trying just to breathe right!
The phlegm in my throat was giving me fright,
My only relief was sitting upright!

Dawn came and went, so did my guest,
As quickly as possible, I be-gan my quest!
I lived near a clinic, so made a request,
For an appointment, to help clear my chest!

Chronic Bronchitis was diagnosed here,
Caused by the dust, no help from the beer!
Introduced to inhalers, my lungs now did clear,
They gave me a scare, yet allowed me some cheer!

Those of us who contract a dread disease like COPD must come to grips with all the really hard questions about life. And, we must identify and deal with the answers as quickly as possible. Under these circumstances, the pressure to achieve the answers adds a lot of pressure and stress to daily living at a time when you can least afford it. While it's not fun, it is essential!

What are your worst fears? How will you deal with them? If your life is suddenly shortened, what decisions will you make about your health, life, family, finances, insurance, car, home, 'toys' and more? When you go to the dentist, will the choices you make be for short-term or long-term care? Do you have a will? Living will? Are you an organ donor? Can or will you do all you can for yourself and your loved ones?

The choices I make for myself may not be the right choices for someone else. Given the chance, how would you counsel another? Given the ailment, how would you deal with these things?

All these and more suddenly stem from one cataclysmic moment. Have you ever wondered how the afflicted felt at the moment of hearing that news?

That Shocking Moment

'Tis hard to explain the shock that you feel,
Upon hearing of diseases no one can heal.
Emphysema is one, made me feel like heel,
Cheating my loved ones, gives them a raw deal!

Doctors may tell you that you have ten years,
Not really knowing how you deal with fears.
Your mind may go numb, eyes well up with tears,
Stomach may flop, knowing 'Your End' appears.

Gasping for air, your blood pressure will rise,
Fears overwhelm; the mouth suddenly dries!
For a few moments, you wrestle with cries,
Disbelieving your ears, then finally realize.

Now your life changes! The choices you make,
Suddenly identify if you're really a flake!
You must have allies to de-lay your wake,
So pull it together, this won't be a clambake!

Fighting to breathe with this dread disease,
Life will continue in spite of my wheeze.
Making new choices, some just to appease,
Activities are cancelled that would really please.

Priorities change; there's less time to make
Decisions about life and things to forsake.
Your health will dictate the pleasures you take,
Best be real careful, can't afford a mistake!

Don't fall apart; there are worse things you see,
I'll do what I must to pursue living by sea.
Scared out of my wits, I seek those who agree,
It's not a death sentence, at least not for me!

The experiences of having COPD are difficult to describe to others. Everyone asks, "How does it feel? What is it like to have COPD? You don't look ill. Can you describe what it's like? Does it hurt? Why can't you sing any more? Are you okay? Why don't you have any energy? Why can't you climb steps? Why can't you attend your favorite event? Why is your color so white? Why are you inside on such a beautiful day?!" Family and friends often ponder or pose these questions as one tries to live and cope with a COPD breathing disorder.

To show someone else how it feels to have a COPD (or similar) breathing disorder is really fairly simple. This actually works (although it may not be the same for all forms of the disease). Have the person place their cupped hand/s over their own mouth and nose. Leave small spaces between the fingers for air. Have them try to breathe easily in that mode. To demonstrate breathing difficulty, close the fingers a little bit and close off the air supply while they try to breathe. That is how it feels to a COPD patient! Oxygen starvation - slow suffocation! It will not take long for them to get the message! You will no longer hear, "I cannot understand it!"

Here is my attempt to provide the answers as I try to describe my form of COPD.

Explain Yourself

How to explain C-O-P-D
To those that I love or caregivers for me.
'Tis hard to describe lung actions that we
are newly learning, without visuals to see.

If you think of lungs as dense sponge full of air,
Everything's fine if you need no repair.
But, if you add water or squeeze without care,
Air space is reduced; oxygen now becomes rare!

The body reacts, to this increased distress,
By raising blood pressure, increasing your stress!
Muscles, brain, organs must now work with less
Oxygen and energy, forcing you to digress!

You're suddenly tired; your body will ache,
Lungs just might hurt; your muscles may shake.
Your energy's gone; some think you're a flake,
Doing much less each day can be hard to take!

Our psyche's bombarded by new efforts made,
To correctly determine what made us afraid!
Now trying harsh meds that once I'd evade,
Can be the difference between living or spade!

Heart, lungs and organs are put to the test,
To help you survive, help you battle this pest.
Medical marvels abound, the diagnosis a quest,
To formulate treatments, re-storing your zest!

The per-va-sive nature, of this dread disease,
Affects the whole body, from mind to your knees.
The meds that we take, trying just to appease,
Have side effects too; aren't used just to please!

Doing simplest of chores or things you adore,
May require oxygen that you cannot ignore!
Singing is out, laughing strikes at your core,
Anything exciting may prompt gasping on floor!

'Tis hard to imagine, sliding into this Hell,
When blood test in twenties, could've foretold this spell.
Now forced to trust others, to help me get well,
I work with caregivers, to restore me to swell.

Oxygenation of blood, is critical each day,
Affects all we do, whether working or play.
Lungs ingest air; meds help us we pray,
The best I can do is fight back all the way.

I have lived most of my life in the abundantly beautiful Northwest corner of the United States. As gorgeous as this region may be, for people who have breathing disorders, this region can have some serious impacts on your health. Most of these are weather or pollution related. Among the weather problems are temperature inversions, heavy doses of pollen or any week where the wind does not blow and the pollutants accumulate. Even driving through an area such as this can be very dangerous for patients of breathing disorders during these particular climatic events.

COPD patients cannot fool around with any of these problems! When your doctor tells you to "Get the heck out of here!" you had better pay close attention. You had also better react as quickly as you can.

Aggravating Changes

Living in apartments that overlooked a lake,
Didn't want to move away, not for any sake.
But if mold is killing you, lakeside you'll forsake,
Preferring my good breathing, rather than my wake!

Rendered nearly useless, my working days are o'er,
Force reliance on my sons, helping with this chore.
Packing is a burden, moving boxes 'round the floor,
Raises fibers I must breath; I dare not open door!

Coughing, wheezing, choking, finally it is done,
Moving to a new place, thank God I had a son!
New place was delightful, sure thought that I had won,
Until my nosebleeds showed, new carpet is no fun!

Formaldehyde replaced mold, killing as before,
Eight months after moving, I'm forced to move once more!
Now we check ev'rything, there's nothing I ignore,
Quickly moving one last time, now we know the score!

Each move has cost a lot, my friends cannot keep track,
Addresses and phone numbers, all are out of whack!
Bank funds near depleted, my meds are in a sack,
Ready if I need them, in case of an attack.

Living standard has declined, but I'm still alive,
Looking forward to the day, when I can survive!
Until that day I must learn to live, love and strive,
Working for better health so once more I can thrive!

When you select or are assigned a Pulmonologist, pay close attention to what he/she tells you. Do not be afraid to ask lots of questions. They have your best interest at heart for both the short and long-term care of your health. However, if the doctor's attitude is not "This does not have to be a death sentence!", go find another doctor. (You can find lists of questions to ask your Pulmonologist at the COPD-International web site.)

The Pulmonologist will give you lots of very good advice. And I will admit, following all their directions is easier said than done!

Scared out of my wits, I have been reading all I can find about this disease called COPD. I want to know exactly what I am up against. While doing that, I am experiencing trauma on a daily basis as I try to breathe and learn to cope with the disease. At this point, all of my senses are being overwhelmed!

While I am trying to learn how to ease my breathing, lessen my pain, clearly identify my new mobility limitations, re-arrange my life schedule and try to stay calm so as not to scare my family, the doctor delivers this very important tidbit of information that goes in one ear and, unfortunately, right out the other. I wish I had slowed it down a bit to grasp more of it for myself when I first heard it.

One Pulmonologist Chant

With C-O-P-D, you will move lots less,
While not what you want, you're forced to digress.
If you eat the same, while in this distress,
The weight that you gain will change how you dress!

You'll blame it on steroids, meds that you use,
While really in truth, most people a-buse!
Food is a comfort, you should not do booze,
While nerves are a wreck, it is hard to snooze!

Your body adjusts, to new meds you take,
The mind keeps on fooling, like it's a fake!
While handling this stress, you now must forsake,
Those large proportions and most of the cake!

Your weight would go up, 'tis bad for your heart,
Breathing gets harder; your organs will smart.
Bowels won't like you, makes foods hard to part,
When held by the body, gases will start!

Drink lots of water. Eat half portions too.
Walk all you can to avoid feeling blue.
Your pulmonary doc, knows what to do,
If you do your share, then they can help you!

Having COPD means that less oxygen is getting to the brain, muscles, organs and all other body parts. Whether you like it or not, you are forced to slow down and do everything at a measured pace. Trying to do anything else is futile. Pacing becomes a coping and survival technique. The sooner you do it, the better you can cope.

One of the major problems with COPD is that you spend so much energy trying to breathe, that you do not have any energy left to do the other things in your life. You do not look ill, but you feel and look lazy to those around you, and to yourself! That poor image works on your mind, your psyche, your family and everyone else around you! Family and friends cannot understand and you do not know how to teach them at this point.

Having failed to implement the proper dietary program, I am beginning to gain weight from lack of activity. The steroid medications help my breathing, but are not helping my weight. I did not know what was really happening, but knew that I was incapacitated, formally disabled and very frustrated because of that incapacitation. Being constantly tired and weary becomes one more frustration that is piled onto the 'frustration pile' you are experiencing. Arguments and short tempers will be added into this volatile mixture.

Adding those frustrations on top of the following frustrations made a very difficult period in the life of this COPD patient!

Frustrations!

Now I must take medicines, for my many ills,
Several are inhalers; many more are pills!
And there are some added chores, managing these hills
Of pills in my cabinet; dealing with the bills!

Inhalers help my breathing, require newfound skills,
Four to six times daily, forgetting will cause thrills!
Water pills drain fluids; prevent my needing gills,
Also keeps my heartbeat, producing just like stills!

Doc told me to avoid stress, moderate my frills,
Control my anxieties; make them all molehills.
Pills help me to handle, I've ordered more refills,
Helps to keep me humming, like fields of whippoorwills.

Apprehension's really tough, much like dental drills,
You know tests are happening, waiting gives me chills!
This process is a coaster, struggling with uphills,
Test results are a rush, like speeding 'round downhills!

Highs, lows, twists, curves, the process forces many spills
Of plans, fun and most things, outside my windowsills.
Breathing hard frustrates me; I'm taking care of wills,
Hope and pray we conquer, before this darn thing kills!

Waiting to find out what is next in the testing cycle for any complex disease can be as difficult as that ailment itself. One becomes dazed, confused and overwhelmed by all the new experiences and terms while trying to learn and understand the disease. Your body rarely cooperates during this time frame. Everything you know to be normal seems to be turned upside down.

There are so many things I would love to do outside. However, I am forced to remain inside, except for very brief outdoor excursions. I am susceptible to just about everything that is airborne. Regardless of that fact, I refuse to let it dampen my spirit.

(This was my first attempt at poetry and my first poem. I have been surprised at how well it was received, surpassing my wildest expectations.)

One Fine Day

The weather outside, it's sunny and bright,
People are playing, they shout with delight,
At a warm springy day, with wonderful sight,
Of birds, trees and grass, impervious to plight.

I ache to be with them, to join in the fun,
To share a few laughs, even throw in a pun.
But, alas I am hostage, as if held by gun,
Ravages of illness prevent fun in the sun.

My breathing is heavy. It's the pollen you see,
Makes my life difficult, coupled with C-O-P-D.
I try just to walk, 'round my pea patch by sea,
Suddenly there's dust! Cruel, how breezes can be.

My weight has gone up, steroid meds they took hold,
Illness kept me inside while the weather was cold.
My health spirals down, I must avoid mold,
Awaiting procedures that can restore me to bold.

To all who might read this, I'd just like to say,
Don't ever try smoking, not even one day.
For sooner or later, you will have to pay,
By watching the others enjoy the fine day.

The life experiences associated with breathing disorders force everyone involved with that patient to become knowledgeable about COPD - a 'forced learning exercise' for patient and family alike. COPD forces you to create a whole new lifestyle. Every day presents something new to learn about and deal with that you were totally unprepared for. It is a whole new ballgame.

One person's joy and delight can instantly become a COPD patient's Achilles heel. This can be devastating to everyone involved – particularly children. Sometimes the simplest thing can be the source of severe reactions!

A Bright Beginning

I awoke today and was feeling real great,
Went for a walk, even kept a blind date.
A thoughtless driver raced by my gate,
Raising clouds of dust, prompting my spate.

Breathing the dust, I coughed, now wheeze,
Wishing for clean air, ten bucks for a breeze!
To blow away dust that was created to please,
The whims of a driver, aimed solely to tease.

Life is so short, its precious you see,
Our health is a blessing. Enjoy it with glee.
Breathing the air is supposed to be free,
When there is dust, sick people must flee.

One day it might be you, enjoying your due,
Catching some fresh air, while just making do,
When suddenly some driver will make ado,
Raising a dust cloud, nearly causing adieu!

Now, drivers don't know, when pleasing their lust,
The damage they'll do, by raising that dust.
For the patients of breathing disorders I must,
Beg your indulgence; avoid dusting our bust!

COPD is a debilitating disease - a curse of sorts. The medications used to treat COPD are great, ease your pain and aide your breathing, but they have one particularly interesting side-affect that can ruin any plans or intentions you may have. And if you are like me (who has now gained 40 pounds), there is almost nothing you can do about it. That impact is the size of your girth!

Women know this from their body activities, but this was a shock to me. My belt line could expand or contract four (4) inches up or down per day! Try as you might, there is almost nothing you can do to control it. At one point, I was buying a new pair of trousers and shirts every month, one size larger than before, just to be able to cope with the problem. Day trips prompt taking two or three sets of clothes along to effectively deal with your ever-changing situation. The expansion and retraction of abdominal girth can be an embarrassing, painful problem!

One event that I really wanted to attend prompted me to buy a new pair of trousers on the way to the event. I was not going to be denied attendance this time! I carefully removed the tags of newness from the pants, put them on and wore them to the festival. Seated in a right side aisle seat, I thoroughly enjoyed the musical event, mingled with the performers and audience when it was over, and later dined with several of them.

Not until I reached home and removed the garment did I realize that I had left the plastic size strip on the pant leg for all to see for the entire time! This 14" strip ran half the length of the pant leg exclaiming my size for all to see!

The Wedding

My son was to marry; the day had been set,
'Twas on Grandpa's birthday, a March day you bet.
Preparations were in order, my son called to fret,
That I needed a tuxedo, to greet guests I met.

All families go through this; it's a really fun deal,
Unless you have illness, that has yet to heal.
For C-O-P-D patients, to display any zeal,
Takes courage, love, strength, guts if you kneel!

As exciting and joyous as the occasion will be,
It's fear of embarrassment that really haunts me.
One effect of the meds used to treat C-O-P-D,
Prompts bloating discomfort, expands what you see!

The stomach can bulge, four inches per day,
Destroying your plans, even dressing for play.
Thoughts of tuxedos, to look good at the fray,
Once fitted right, could burst while you pray!

We went to the fitting, to see what they had,
Fearful, yet hopeful, that it would not be bad.
To my delight, they had clothes that fit Dad,
Any shape I developed, elastic kept me in fad!

We met for this gala, dressed up for their do,
To celebrate happiness, the starting of two!
We took time to honor, grandpa's 94th too,
Toasting the 'Old Goat', please pass a brew!

The wedding is over; we had a great time,
Took many pictures, they all turned out fine.
Looking back on the joy, I grin while opine,
'Bout unfounded fears, while sipping my wine!

With diseases of the lung, you quickly learn (some more quickly than others) that you cannot do all of the things you would like to do. In fact, there are many things you love to do that you just no longer can participate in: social activities, family festivities, attending movies, festivals and oh, so many more things. One reason for these limitations is that you almost always need immediate access to your medications in the event of a flare up.

You also learn to enjoy every moment of good time that you have. Cherish and love it, for the odds are that it will not last for very long. You quickly learn to 'live in the moment', as fleeting as that may be. You learn to grasp and cling to every bit of positive you can find. Sometimes we are not sure what those positive elements are at the moment, but we gain vision from our hindsight. Every now and then you forget yourself and get carried away by the joy of the moment, a great sunny spring day or some other attraction you love.

A Silver Lining

The day was magnificent! We had many plans.
Spring filled the air. We contemplated tans!
Living with C-O-P-D, I also celebrate the sans,
Of allergies, dust, pollen and burning bans.

Car loaded we drove, to share this great day,
Of shopping, lunch, movie, just trying to play.
We luckily parked, without having to pay,
There's even a chance, to see new grandson Clay!

We'd heard on the radio, the weather was fine,
But cautioned of inversions and pollen of pine.
We shopped until three then took time to dine,
As pollen overwhelmed me, like crushing a vine!

We scrambled to car, medicating with a pair
Of meds I must carry for lungs that need air.
My color turned white, I suddenly knew to repair
To a different location where air would be fair!

We drove forty minutes, scurrying from town,
Partner now frightened, observing with frown.
C-O-P-D patients cannot play like a clown,
If dangers of pollen prompt shutting lungs down!

Until we get ill, we don't know living on dole,
Or forsaken joys, singing 'round barber pole,
Of family, work, fun, why I can't even bowl!
So now I write poems, with my heart and soul!

There are times when we are our own worst enemy! If we try to do too much or ignore our illness, even for just a little bit, our circumstances can get out of hand in a hurry. It gets very scary and expensive when things (that you are able to control) are allowed to get out of hand. What's more, when you get frightened, you do not think clearly, do not remember the right meds you can take for various situations (from among 20+) and you make foolish choices.

Two over the counter (OTC) antihistamine tablets might have prevented this episode.

Independence Day

We'd had a great fourth, socializing with zeal,
Enjoyed family 'n friends, had a great meal.
Sipping on white wine, the weather ideal,
As final guests left, lungs forced me to kneel!

I'd felt pressure building, ignored the increase
Of breathing problems or a chance to decease!
Lung meds had helped, but pressure didn't cease,
Suddenly I'm frightened, began packing valise!

Now seated at computer, I typed out my will,
Made lists of my meds, wrote check for a bill.
Sleepless all night writing instructions with quill,
For family to follow if I went downhill!

As morning arrived, I'm having a bad day,
Was admitted to hospital, testing ability to pay.
Two-thousand bucks later, I went my way,
With a new worry, to find that much hay!

Pollen had dropped me, but I didn't know,
That I had the meds to pre-vent that blow!
Antihistamines worked, allowed air to flow,
If I had thought, could've saved all that dough!

COPD made lungs sensitive to air,
Filled with weed pollen, floating 'round there.
'Twas revelation for me that gave me a scare,
In spite of great docs, I'm in charge of my care!

Here is an interesting thought. We are all addicted to two things in life - air and water! You simply cannot live without them.

As breathing gets more difficult for COPD patients, we are forced to consider (plead for) the use of oxygen to supplement what we normally breathe. Oxygen therapy is prescribed by the primary care doctor; usually a Pulmonologist. Each specific breathing condition will dictate the specific form of oxygen therapy patients will receive. Sleep apnea is completely different from emphysema, which is very different from asthma, or black lung disease, etc. There are oxygen therapies tailored to each affliction.

Oxygen is a mixed blessing for COPD patients. While helping you breathe easier, it also forces the patient to develop a new way of living – coping with the paraphernalia associated with oxygen. In addition, oxygen encourages flammables, thereby forcing the patient to be extremely wary of dangerous situations and to avoid smoking at all costs. It truly is a new way of life.

New Way Of Living

To look at me there's nothing wrong, it's all inside you see,
But once you hear me laugh, you experience fragile me.
Lungs will not support my voice; scarcely express my glee,
Enjoying another glorious day or breathing air that's free.

I'm labeled as disabled, there's a placard on my dash,
Another in my wallet accompanies dwindling cash.
I park near doors, walk real slow, 'dash' from sash to sash,
Because cold air or pollen, may cause my lungs to crash!

Primary doctor ordered tests, to see how I would fare,
Determining how he'll proceed, with my path of care.
CAT scans, x-rays, EKGs, blood tests by the pair,
Cardiograms, PFTs, treadmills tattle my despair.

Walking measured course today, to test my oxygen rate,
Checking heart 'n lung capacity, from start to finish gate.
Meters check my blood gas-es, to see if I deflate,
Ideal is ninety-five percent, I'm gasping at eighty-eight!

Now I must have oxygen, to help me every day,
Compressor form, liquid form, portable for 'play',
Tethered by my air hoses, 'tis living a whole new way!
Alas, it beats the alternative of watching family pray!

Prescribed oxygen is delivered in primarily two forms - liquid and compressed, using several pieces of equipment for delivery directly to the patient. My emphysema based COPD prompted the more common form of oxygen therapy, so now I must learn how to live with it. I will tell you that it is another major lifestyle undertaking. You will have these for the rest of your life, so get used to them.

I consider these tanks of liquid and compressed oxygen to be an external lung. Learning how to live and cope with this new extremity can be daunting! Among the most common difficulties associated with oxygen is learning how to cope with and handle the 50-foot feeder line that tethers you to the home equipment. My ears, nose and head have been jerked around so many times that I think I have permanent whiplash!

Still, more interesting challenges are sleeping, showering or using the restroom with the cords. Aside from the benefit of breathing better, the other advantage is that everyone knows where you are – at the other end of the line!

Commercial travel, particularly air travel, can be an expensive, logistical nightmare! Airlines treat your equipment as an explosive, so they will not allow it on the airplane. While there are ways to deal with it, the patient must make all the arrangements. Always check with you insurance provider for answers.

Watch Your Feet!

Living with my oxygen, newly part of me,
Like a new external lung, lets me breathe with glee!
While it helps my breathing, 'tis curse for moving free,
It's a real mixed blessing, I'm sure you will agree.

Compressor oxygen is used while I'm homebound,
Tethered to just fifty feet, cord lays on the ground.
Others trip upon my cord, jerk my head around,
Giving me a whiplash, prompts me to rebound!

My ears and nose are battered; tears have run from eyes,
Ears were nearly ripped from head, trusting my cord ties!
Humidity and stress, prompt usage that relies,
On more volume from the tank, struggling for new highs!

Going out in public, allows me to feel free,
'Tis a hassle getting there: sometimes takes a plea!
First I fill my portable, grab the meds for me,
Loading them in the car, I head for store or sea.

Enjoying each new outing, freedom lights my face,
Fills my heart with gratitude, grinning like an ace!
Breathing time is limited, but I will not race,
30-Gallon car tank, refills me any place!

Walking with my oxygen, sometimes in a cart,
Cann-u-la in my nose, it is no piece of art!
Little children point and stare, parents will depart,
Steering them away from me, like I fired a fart!

Tra-ve-ling can be a pain; flying is no fun,
Airports view our oxygen, just like we had gun!
You must make arrangements, for oxy in the sun,
Flying trips all 'round our world, costs will really stun!

Now you know some joys of life, living with canned air,
I can tell you with chagrin, breathing here is rare!
Given the alternatives, I dare to compare,
All those little tragedies, with each breath so fair!

Thirteen months of testing are nearly complete. I have learned a lot, but there is much more to know. I have experienced a lot, hurt a lot, been truly frightened several times and been aggravated when some of my tests became outdated before decisions could be made.

Aggravating as this may be, now I must repeat one of my tests and have positive results in order to get the referral I need to the surgery team. My primary/pulmonary doctor has ordered the test and, when completed, I will meet with him for his final decision. Personal tensions are high.

Clinging to every ray of hope, I have steadfastly maintained my positive attitude that I will somehow manage to get through this and become a viable candidate for an LVRS (Lung Volume Reduction Surgery) operation. Less than 1% of all COPD patients can qualify for the open chest version of the LVRS operation. Except for my lung problem, the rest of my health must be nearly perfect in every respect. (There is also a laser version of LVRS that deals with smaller portions of the lung. The physical requirements are less stringent.)

Anxious Moment

There have been many tests; now the moment draws near,
When I'll learn the answers to my worries and fear.
My health has been declining; I am of good cheer,
Waiting my referral to their surgery peer!

Qualifying here requires health be the best,
In every department except lungs in your chest!
Your heart must be strong; blood flow cannot be a pest,
If you hope to gain a chance to restore your zest!

Echocardiogram test checks beats of your heart,
Taking many close looks, at my heart's every part.
Pillows press to my back, my left side's on a cart,
Operator tells me when she's ready to start.

She passes a wand o'er, the best place on my chest,
To get the clearest pictures, sounds and all the rest.
Now monitoring blood, each valve's a flipping test,
Functions are recorded, the video attests!

Meeting with my doctor, he's double-checked all chores,
He's looked at the video, triple-checked all scores.
He sets surgeon appointment; my heart really soars,
Then he wishes me well and I glide through the doors!

From earliest childhood, I had always been dressed well. Mom saw to that, even though I was my father's boy.

As a business professional, I always felt comfortable in a suit, shirt and tie (well, the tie was part of the uniform). Now that I am ill, no longer able to work and forcibly retired due to my disability, I have had trouble dressing correctly. My choice of clothing just has not seemed to work for me. The various medical conditions I find myself in, particularly as it related to the medical staff and what they might ask of me, are all new to me. However, be assured that I am a quick study!

Dressing For Success

Surgeons set my appointment, a consult they say,
And said "On your way in stop to get an X-ray."
I arrived and parked early, not sure where I'd stray,
Wandering large hospital this wonderful day.

Nuclear Medicine 'waited, just like it's mapped,
I quipped with the lady, "I'm ready to be zapped."
She told me, "Just take a seat. Try not to get flapped.
A tech will come get you and you will be unwrapped!"

Techs led me to X-ray, 'twas exactly at two.
She said "Take off your shirt and your undershirt too!
Let the suspenders hang low, don't wanna see through
Nothing but lungs and those curly hairs too!"

With hands in my pockets, I pressed shoulders to plate,
Set my chin on the top as she shouted, "Inflate!"
Picture now taken she says "Turn right my dear mate.
Both hands grab the high bar." I now knew my fate!

Protesting my dropped pants, she said, "Don't be in fear,
I've seen it before. I promise I will not leer!"
Assuming the position, my chest was now clear,
My pants dropped to the floor, exposing what's dear!

This awkward exposure did not last very long,
Taught me some lessons about things I had done wrong.
All my future x-rays found me humming a song,
Dressed in a sweat suit, smugly grinning along!

With diseases like COPD, you simply cannot attend the functions or festivities you would like. Due to the disease, there are now so many things that can impact you that you may become frightened of doing anything at all. Suddenly, this previously gregarious, outgoing, fun-loving person had become a stay at home 'shut-in' for fear of what might happen.

Usually the precautions are well founded. The least little thing can trigger an episode of severe bronchitis, an asthma attack or just make my breathing difficult. Climbing a few steps or some stairs, walking any distance, doing anything strenuous, a cold blast of wind, or worst of all, belly laughing as you enjoy something really funny can be instantly debilitating.

Due to these fears and this kind of reaction to the disease, I missed several events that were very important to me: the funeral of my step-dad, family events and this special moment.

Celebrating One!

Clayton Tanner Vogel celebrates one year today,
He's bound to have toys, with which to play.
So my contribution, are words cast for Clay,
In hopes of your happiness, on this joyous day.

As proud as Grandfathers, are likely to be,
It's hovering Grandmothers, who want to hold ye!
Some family and friends, will do honor to thee,
But, Grandson I'm sorry, that it cannot be me.

Today I am with you, just in spirit you see,
My heart fills with gladness just knowing you'll be,
Surrounded by loved ones, that's your family tree,
Who celebrate birthdays, with your family of three.

Happy Birthday my grandson, there'll be many more.
For now enjoy family and your friends who adore.
My small gift for savings, is delivered to the door,
Of your mom and dad's house, given with amore!

Hopes are high, attitude is good, I am in the final stages of selection for an operation that I want to help my breathing. The last thing I want to hear is "we have a problem".

I am ready. I know I am! Except for my lungs, my health is excellent. However, the doctors must be certain that, before they operate, I will have the best possible chance of survival and recovery that is possible. We all know there are no guarantees. Aggravating as this moment can be, they are probably correct, but what a time to decide this! I just want to get on with it!

We Have A Problem

Pulmonary diseases are something scary indeed,
Require attentions and services of a new breed.
Medical professionals and my family all agreed,
To work with the problem to get my breathing freed.

I've met with the surgeons, there's a problem to check,
A question of heart valve that may stick a speck!
It must be correct or my plans are a wreck,
So exploratory surgery must check with a trek.

Admitted to the hospital, pre-op meds are a chore,
But they facilitate surgery on the third floor.
Next morning I wake, surrounded by four
Guys who are saying, we're ready to explore!

Anesthetic allows them to do what they need,
Without fear of pain, I can watch as they feed.
Camera and wire make a pinky sized lead,
Trekking through veins, to see my blood speed.

From thigh past my groin, the camera is fed,
Then zips past my tummy, I don't feel a thread.
Finally reaching my heart, quipping operator said,
"Aha! I see the valve and it looks bloody red!"

For nearly ten minutes, the camera stays there,
Recording valve functions, with nary a glare.
The videotape record is now ready to share,
With docs who make calls, about my healthcare!

A few hours later, I am homeward bound,
To wait for results of what surgery found.
One week would pass before phone made a sound,
To schedule my visit and, boy, am I wound!

Every person I have encountered with breathing disorders has had one or more days where they were remorseful/regretful for their behavior; living conditions, etc. Each one longs to turn back the clock to a better day, willing to do almost anything to correct their condition or find a new resolution to their dilemma. I am no exception.

Short of that, I have chosen to write about all these illness elements in hopes that I can shed light for others and ease their burden. In this way I hope to turn those remorseful feelings and thoughts into something positive. Going through the process, I have gained a new, deeper understanding of 'enjoy the moment'. It's all we really have.

Savoring Life

I have lived my life full, always doing my best,
Thrilled with each moment, barely took time to rest.
I counted my blessings, enjoyed many a fest,
Loving art 'n music, made many a request.

The joy of the people, I found at those places,
Could lift people up, from the darkest of spaces.
Skills honed to perfection, reflect in the faces,
Of artisans showing all manner of graces.

I am strong in conviction, in Faith and in hope,
I'm thankful for all things that help me to cope.
But foremost of all, I stopped being a dope,
When offered tobacco, I now tell them nope!

With diseases of lung, your life turns on a dime,
Affects loved ones a lot, your ability to rhyme.
All things you would do to express your good time,
Can suddenly force, communication like mime!

I don't know one person, with an illness like mine,
Who would not trade it all for the chance to opine
Of breathing freely again for family fine,
Or doing fun things that make our life so divine.

The time for final operational decisions has arrived. After 16 months, the tests are complete (some two or three times). Doctors have scrutinized the x-rays, the charts, my vital signs, weight, done exploratory surgery to examine a heart valve and know everything medically about me. Except for my emphysema and its impact on my body, I am in perfect health! How ironic that sounds!

In previous conversation, surgeons have discussed with me that LVRS operations are 'quality of life' operations, not life saving operations. There are no guarantees. I understand that, if successful, this operation can help me live a better life for 3-6 years, maybe less, maybe more. Beyond that time frame is anyone's guess. I understand and readily accept these facts. I have shared them with my family and friends. We await the final decision of the surgeons.

Roll God's Dice

Summoned to the hospital, I eagerly wait my fate,
Sixteen months of testing prompted me to spate!
Dreaded fateful meetings, may best be done sans mate,
Truth is often shocking, prompts many mates to hate!

Seated among the afflicted, most are worse than me,
Blessings known, I commiserate with tobacco legatee.
Vital signs get taken; I've gained another three,
Impacting lifestyle quality, threatening what may be!

Ushered to surgery sanctum, now seated in the room,
Tobacco habits tattle, 'tis 'qualified' or 'doom'.
Resisting fears of horror or scurrying to my tomb,
Exuding vim and vigor, I'll ride out on my broom!

Thoracic surgeons explain to me, every LVRS detail,
Risks to life and living, happenings if they fail.
Actions here reduce disease, remove tissues into pail,
Staple, seal, lungs 'n chest, hopefully we shout Hail!

Qualified when hundreds can't, my choice is made to win.
Loving music, family, nature, art and performances akin,
That stimulate humorous senses, while teasing with a grin!
Life's so great, let's roll God's dice, I'm ready to begin!

LVRS operation Details: I checked into the hospital October 7th (in time for dinner), received my pre-op medications from the staff and retired for the night. I vaguely remember hearing someone tell me "we will see you on the other side" at about 5AM and that was it!

The open chest LVRS operation (like open heart surgery) removed the upper 1/3 of both lungs, sealed both lungs, installed drain plugs, tied my sternum together with a steel cable and then closed my skin over that. The entire process lasted just short of 2 hours.

Because I was 'out of it' during the operation, the details of the operation and the immediate follow-on events could only be related by someone else – my mom, a sweetheart, etc.

This poem recounts a sweetheart's story of those events. I do not remember any of them myself. I wrote the poem based upon her tale of events and applied her personality in the process. With her approval, it is written in the first person, as if she were telling you the story.

Loved One's Viewpoint

A loved one in surgery, is not any fun,
When you must wait, worrying a ton!
At last surgeons tell me, "He really has won,
You'll see him shortly, the worst is now done".

I worried and waited, seemed forever to me,
Finally walked to the counter, so mad I could pee!
Wanting to see him, I buzzed loudly with glee,
Then let myself in, headed straight to see Lee.

He sat in a chair, as I entered the door,
Many were scurrying, medical staff there galore!
Four tubes in his chest, hung down to the floor,
Draining fluids of surgery, I could only deplore.

A sight to behold, doctors scolded a nurse,
She had over-sedated and could not reverse!
Life hung in the balance, so I shouted sans verse,
"Wake up you old goat or I'll give you a curse!"

His eyes popped wide open, just fearing the worst,
While still in his stupor, he spoke with lips pursed.
"It hurts!" he said wincing, docs scrambled and cursed,
Shouting "Keep him awake! We'll get this reversed!"

Seated beside him, I looked at his welt,
Heard his complaints, empathized what he felt.
'Twas his first operation and yes, a real belt,
Then recalled seven births, the hand I'd been dealt.

I said "Tomorrow you'll forget, while eating a cookie."
"Wanna bet?!", he retorted, "I'm playing hooky!"
Now medicated, sleeping, he sounded like wookie!
This guy's had it too good. Why, he's just a rookie!

The LVRS operation is done! In my case, surgeons opened my chest, placed a clamp between the good and bad parts of each lung, stapled it in place and then cut off the bad lung tissue. I refer to the process as a 'medical seal-a-meal'. The operation removed about 1/3 of each lung.

Now I start my recovery. If all of the pre-operation test results were accurate, I should do well. However, everyone is different and each body reacts differently to these kinds of stress and trauma. Time, my body and its proper care will determine the outcome.

As one who has never been seriously ill one day in his life, these experiences are a major learning exercise! I had visited others in hospitals, but never been a patient and never really understood what my family or friends had gone through. How naive! How little I knew! Empathy begins with experience!

ICU

Oh, man, oh man! My op-er-ation's done!
Chest pain and recovery have only just begun!
Twenty-one days assistance, expected 'til I shun,
These sterile halls of medicine, in favor of some sun!

Now in Ward called ICU, they watch me like a hawk,
Round the clock attention, for my every squawk.
Sedated with these heavy meds, I cannot even talk,
Barely know what's happenin', mouth tastes just like chalk!

Fluids drain from my chest to bags hung near the floor,
Monitors beep in my ear, keep nurses near my door.
Food and meds feed through tubes, hard to know the score,
Clutching red heart pillow, to visitors I'm a bore!

Fourth day turns brighter as my body really heals,
They pull the drains, get me up, set me on new wheels.
Meds ease off, head clears some, I chat in little squeals,
Incision healing, docs are happy with lung seals.

Fifth day is exciting, they walk some steps with me,
Trailing meds along, I am shuf-fl-ing with Bea.
Once I walk just fifty feet, they will set me free,
Leaving ICU and on to Re-cov-er-y!

Able to communicate, I share how I feel,
Tell of sternum movements, in spite of woven steel.
Cable is required, to help incisions seal,
'Tis so thin I wont know, wont cause an airport squeal.

Doctors are amazed as, day seven dawns all 'round,
Healing has advanced and I'm walking all around!
Healing progress lets me move, I'm recovery bound,
Promising some new friends and real food to be found!

I have been in recovery for a total of nine days now. Each day I have gotten stronger, dealt better with the heavy medications, steadily improved my sleep, walked further and generally began to feel better. However, there are a few things that are not back to normal.

Heavy surgical medications just absolutely obliterate your taste buds, senses and body functions. The senses will eventually return, but a sure sign of your improvement is when you begin to eat again. That is the point where you begin to demonstrate one body function to your caregivers.

For the nine days of recovery preceding this one, the only things I could eat from my plates were fruit cups. They were the only things with a decently strong flavor that I could both taste and enjoy! Then there was this moment of epiphany.

Epiphany Of My Recovery

I woke with the sun shining bright in my face,
It's my favorite way, no matter what place.
Peace of the moment exploded from trace,
"Top o' the mornin'! bellowed he, sans any grace.

Aids scurried behind, in the shadow of Bear,
Dispensing medications, with minimal flare.
We dealt with essentials, then awaited our fare,
Expecting good meals prepared with great care.

Now I'm no complainer, 'cause I've just been saved,
But man I'd been starving, while others had raved!
Food quality was great. Hospital staff had behaved,
But escaping medical stupor left me feeling depraved!

Medication alters taste buds, favorite things you adore,
Look great when delivered, but tastes like the floor!
Nine days and nights trying, tasting flavors I deplore,
But, tonight it was different; salvation entered my door.

My son and his family, using grandson as guise,
Produced watermelon slices, an incredible prize!
My eyes opened wide, senses rose in surprise,
The lust for this flavor, I could not disguise!

Holding these morsels, I caressed each curved rind,
Eyes dancing o'er seeds, like peeking through blind.
My nose twitched with glee upon smelling their kind,
While tongue moistened lips, stimulated my mind!

To my delight, they offered salt for this meat,
Which I joyfully sprinkled, preparing to eat.
Lifting first piece to mouth, was really a feat,
Fearing taste bud rejection would be defeat!

The melon tip passed, just be-tween lips,
When tongue came in contact, I tightened my grips!
Melon flavor filled mouth; my chest caught the drips,
I could not have cared less what it did to my hips!

They chatted. I snacked, savoring bites like a prize!
Tasty slice was just great, didn't matter what size!
Devouring the second, was a de-lightful reprise,
Making melon feast equal, the morning sunrise.

After they'd gone, I'd thanked them for mine,
While settling to bed, was prepared to recline.
In spite of chest pains, it had been a great dine,
'Twas then that I knew, I was going to be fine!

As a first time hospital patient, I admit that I was green as grass. I did not know the things that govern patient movement from place to place, what things prompt decisions about me or the things that would get me released to go home again.

I had been so involved with learning about COPD, learning how to cope with my disease, plus getting selected and preparing for my LVRS surgery, that I never gave a thought to the events or circumstances that follow the operation; much less ask the proper questions so that I was a knowledgeable patient. Lack of knowledge can be very frustrating and aggravating as your days in recovery pass. However, with patience, a good attitude, determination, a little bit of luck, a good hospital staff and the help of an unsung hero, I made it just fine!

Unsung Hero

Serious operations, will change your mind about,
Things we call miracle or postures you may tout.
Heavy meds you're given, to get you through this bout,
Bring insightfulness of caregivers and devout.

Pre-op meds will change your bod, stop your bowels dead,
Interrupt your functions; prompt everything you dread!
Part of your recov'ry means eating what you're fed,
Also passing all the stuff, making your face red!

Ten days with no movement, means pains not Heaven sent,
Enema's suggested, 'tis a bles-sed event!
Abdomen's been bloated, the body wants to vent,
Chest pains take a back seat, to pains I wish were spent!

Doubled over in pain, I ring caregiver aid,
To relieve the strain, for which enemas are made!
With application done, from my sight does she fade,
I in turn relieve my stress! Hope she is well paid.

That was the final test, for me to be released,
Demonstrating functions, to staff that has policed.
Next day they'd send me home, happily not deceased,
Ent'ring home recov'ry, sans pain that has now ceased.

Counseling with pharmacist, meds he teaches me,
Showing off mobility, therapists agree.
Clutching red heart pillow, my attitude is glee,
Thankful Aides 'n enemas, really set me free!

Eleven days after the operation I was released from the hospital and allowed to go home. That was a new recovery record for an open chest LVRS operation, breaking the old record by six days. University of Washington/VA physicians jokingly proclaimed me their 'Poster Boy'!

Not really knowing exactly what going home entailed, and still under the influence of the heavy drugs, I was eager! Funny how your mind can delude you! Having demonstrated mobility, body function and the basic ability to care for myself without passing out from the pain, they provided me with all the meds I would need (with proper instruction) and sent me on my way.

There are changes that are simply impossible to prepare for: altered taste buds, effects of medications, new medications, doing normal chores or tasks like going to the bathroom, keeping yourself clean and trying not to be a burden to your loved ones. Chest pains are with you every step of the way day and night.

Add to those things the dangers of medications that can become habit forming while you also manage your pain, try to get a full night's sleep, do some daily exercises and, ultra important, avoid water retention (edema can cause congestive heart failure, heart attack or stroke)! LVRS is not recommended for the faint of heart. But, what a joy to get past the milestone of LVRS and rejoin the living!

Taking Charge

Home from the hos-pi-tal, adjustments hard to make,
Hospital bed was offered; my declining was mistake.
Biggest change is sleeping, each odd hour I'm awake,
Rising from my tummy, creates a small earthquake!

Left leg follows right leg till my knees are on the floor,
Gently shifting weight now, I'm avoiding pains galore!
Kneeling by the bed, torso's balanced by all four,
I gently shift to stand erect, am headed for the door.

Whether potty break or medicine, each rising takes a toll,
To satisfy the body's needs, becomes your total role.
Shuf'ling through the house at night, I satisfy each goal,
Then back to bed is easy with a gentle body roll.

Managing meds is difficult, there's many more you see,
Using Morphine, Oxycodin and antibiotics by decree!
Pain management is easy, to make a happy me,
Weaning now is crucial, to stay addiction free!

Follow-up visit to the doc, shows everything is jake,
I'm on the road to recovery; someone pass the cake!
Strongest flavored foods are best, the others I forsake,
Sleeping habits settle down, four hours 'til I wake.

Three to four weeks later, my body's settled down,
Taste buds are recovering, I'm moving like a clown.
I've lost my taste for coffee, am dining with a frown,
My exercise is walking, but I dare not go to town.

Six weeks now, I can drive, my chest still hurts a bit,
It's a real mixed blessing, not meant for any twit!
Thanksgiving is fam'ly day we gather round the spit,
My brother leads the cooking while I just mainly sit.

We talk of my procedures; I get to show my scar,
Chat of my precautions that protect me from a jar.
'Tis the first time in two years I've traveled very far,
Joining family who in turn, make me feel like star!

Surgery pain's subsided; coughs 'n hiccups are a trip,
I cling to red heart pillow, with a real good grip!
Chest pain may be felt one year, while I regain my zip,
Lots of rest helps attitude, 'tis required if you quip!

Praise to my caregiver, who put up with this mess,
She handled me with kindness, in spite of all the stress.
Fighting problems of her own, her care was never less,
Always there for my needs, sure hope the Lord will bless!

Before my LVRS surgery, I could not be outside if the temperature was below 45 degrees, regardless of the humidity factor. The pain created by the cool air on my lungs was akin to holding your hand in the flame of a burning candle. You could not do it very long and it hurts like the Devil! Serious damage can result – quickly!

Now I must begin to see if the surgery has helped me cope with this problem or not. The surgeons gave me no guarantees of success. They told me that it would take up to one year from the surgery date to truly know whether the surgery had been successful or not. My total functionality would become the true test.

Total functionality begins with small steps. Using all due precautions, I will test myself to see what improvements resulted from the surgery. Here was my first test in 41-degree weather.

The Morning Dew

Weary of being in the house, I'll stroll outside to see,
What the impact on my lungs, the new fall air will be.
Sun is shining, dew remains, blue-jays pound oak tree,
Grabbing acorns from the moss, off they fly with glee!

Mask in hand, I walk outside to test my breathing skill,
On this cool fall morning while breezes re-main still.
Grasping squeegee for my car, it really is a thrill,
To simply clean the windows, in the morning chill.

Walking 'round the car I see, a doe with two small deer,
Grazing in the grass nearby, not even showing fear.
Pausing to enjoy this sight, my breathing I can hear,
Phlegm has prompted wheezing, so my throat I must clear.

Coughing to dislodge the mass, sounds disturb this sight,
Deer dart over riverbank, then feed to their delight.
Cool air has not hurt me, my breathing is alright,
So I return to clearing dew, in the morning light.

The joy of breathing without pain, is blessing enough for me,
Although it's only temporary, I do everything with glee!
The surgery didn't save my life; it only set me free,
Giving me a few more years, enjoyment by the sea.

Fighting breathing disorders can lead to a depressed state of mind at various stages of the disease for a wide variety of reasons. It is like being forced to take the worst roller-coaster ride of your life!

One way I always managed to keep a positive attitude and my spirits high was to recall the great things that had happened in my life. I have been fortunate to have a great number of good things to recall — singing barbershop music with a bunch of great guys, traveling every corner of North America, having a good family, achieving great pioneering things in my professional life, enjoying people, golfing, becoming a pilot, family events, plus this very exciting, very special day.

Favorite Father's Day

When you get ill, thoughts turn to the past,
Of family activities, with frequent repast,
To memories of fun and moving real fast,
Just doing together, the real things that last.

Dan was provider of my best Father's Day,
Aided by siblings who showed up to play.
They coaxed me to dress, prepare for a day,
Of excitement and fun, refused my nay say!

Hi-jacked for the day, Debi drove her small car,
In a direction unusual, so it wasn't for par!
Boys squeezed in the back, my head cleared the bar,
Sticking through sunroof, hopefully not far!

Dan made arrangements, to fly with The Boys,
Known as Red Barons, in their marvelous toys!
Excitement leaped high, ent'ring this airfield of joys,
Where Stearmans were parked, eager with poise!

Instructed in 'chutes, the equipment and pace,
My barnstorming gear dons firmly in place!
Now seated in cockpit, big grin on my face,
One last hurrah with flight's freedom and grace.

Seatbelt and straps, tightened and checked,
Red Baron tests comm gear, "Ready?!" he asked.
Thumbs up, I reply, when I ought to be gassed,
To quell my excitement, the adrenaline massed!

We taxied in pairs, these Red Barons and I,
Lined up on the runway, in formation to fly.
Engines roar as we roll, "Smoke on!" flying by,
While Debi took pictures, we jumped to the sky!

Flying south to a mountain, 'tis Rainier in the sun,
We'll do aerobatics, where real wings get won!
The wind whips my cheeks, while preparing to run,
Through glorious maneuvers, pilots call fun!

Ten minutes we flew, toward snowcapped Rainier,
When Red Baron began, calling moves in my ear.
We loop, roll and turn, without any fear,
Gravity, skill, harness prevent falling from here!

Snowcapped Rainier, zips through my sight,
With every maneuver, inverted and upright.
With snap-rolls real sharp, figure-eights tight,
Tailspins and dives made a magnificent flight!

Euphoria complete, we turn to-ward base,
While other Red Barons, quickly gave chase.
Sharing the controls, I flew my own pace,
Heart filled with joy, huge grin on my face!

Landing was perfect, I stepped from the plane,
Glanced quickly inside, to check for a stain!
Handshakes 'n thanks to these Daredevils main,
Hugs for my children, for this memory gain!

There's nothing to replace that wonderful joy,
Of being with family and playing with toy.
Take time for your loved ones, it really is poi,
Food for your soul, you will always enjoy!

While many who have LVRS operations are able to get up and go 'full tilt' immediately after their operation, I was not that lucky. Following my operation, I needed to have Pulmonary Rehabilitation. I recommend it highly to every COPD patient!

Struggling to find accessible services close to where I lived was one problem. Getting it paid for was another. Once I determined that insurance (Medicare) would cover most of the costs, I embarked upon another new adventure.

Huffin' 'n Puffin'

Man, I'm feelin' lucky! My oper-ation's done!
Breathing now is easier. I even shared a pun!
Work begins anew, if I'm to have some fun,
Golfing, loving, teasing, enjoying what I've won.

I requested rehab; they sent me to St Pete,
Where Pulmonary Rehab, means walking on your feet!
Plugged into a computer, that monitors each beat,
Watched over by a therapist who will not let me cheat!

Walking for my health, I'm prodded and I'm poked,
Encouraged to get better by a therapist who's stoked!
My vital signs get taken, confirming I'm not choked,
From huffin' 'n puffin' efforts or the ego he has stroked!

Thirty minutes later, when I'm ready for some rest,
My therapist encourages, "Progress to be your best!"
Sipping juices in between, we move on to a test,
Where aerobics build my stamina, expanding my big chest.

Pulling weights, lifting weights, leg lifts on machine,
I guard against eruptions from, my lunch with a bean!
Finally leaving ol' St Pete, I will take time to preen,
Reminded of my Honor Guards, when I was Marine.

Twice a week for eighteen weeks, insurance has expired,
My need goes on to exercise, the skills that I've acquired.
I'll use my home equipment now, to see if I get wired,
To follow all the teachings, that my therapist inspired.

And so the final test is set, that measures me to task,
My exercise 'n breathing work, can't hide behind a mask.
Spirit, meds, desires prompt, accomplishment sans bask,
My medical teams have given me, all that I could ask

There are interesting side effects to some of the medications we use to ward off COPD. In my case, one side effect was the same before the LVRS operation as it is after the operation. This particular side effect is not caused so much by the medicine itself, but rather by the build-up of the medications in our systems over time.

While my medications are basically the same now as they were before the operation (this may not be true for everyone), the difference is that there are far fewer recurrences of these side effects since having the operation. Believe me, that is a blessing!

Wee Hour Surprises

I'd had a good day, our mood had been right,
Enjoyed a fun nooner that brought us delight.
Took all the meds prescribed for my plight,
Worked at my writing late into the night.

Retiring at midnight, I was a bit late,
Fell asleep in an instant, be-side my mate.
Then suddenly at three, as if bit by snake,
I leaped from my bed with a terrible spate!

Leg muscles were cramping, knotted real tight,
Caused heart-stopping pain, giving me fright!
I stumbled around, grumbling loud in the night,
While walking it off, I made quite a sight!

So now I own tools, that help me stem pain,
When cramps come around, in spite of the rain.
Putting feet on foot rollers, by chair I do gain
Relief for my pain; some control of domain.

The meds that we take, fighting COPD,
Have side effects too, causes cramping in me.
Sometimes a foot, toes or legs it may be,
You never know, what'll wake you at three!

'Tis usually at night, in spite of quinine
That I take for relief, each night after nine.
This occasional stress, that prompts me to whine,
Is small consolation, for breathing so fine!

Identified as something of a renaissance man by friends, I was involved in a great many things before contracting COPD. With the ailment having a negative, assertive influence on the body, one is forced to make life changes whether you like them or not.

I've said it before, but let me say it again: some things become virtually impossible to do, regardless of how badly you wish to do them. The simple things like enjoying warm, fragrant spring days, doing simple fun things with family or friends like kite flying, going to a movie and many others can all become a burden to you and those around you. No matter how badly you try to prevent it, the ailment will impact everyone in your realm.

People rarely understand why you have the difficulties you do. As victims of breathing disorders, one thing we must do is convince those around us that we have learned from our experiences, that we are able to make the right choices for ourselves and be involved (or not) with those things we are able to cope with and handle. That can be an interesting, ongoing task.

Everyday Choices

With breathing disorders, life can be a thrill,
When weather's not good or if there's a chill.
Everyday things, once loved can now kill,
Just struggling to do, requires oxy or pill.

Simplest of pleasures, we all took for granted,
Now become scary, prompt de-cisions slanted.
Shopping, parties, working in a yard planted,
Are subject to cautions, of what doctors chanted.

C-O-P-D patients know that dangers abound
From normal activity like flying from ground!
Each takeoff, flight, landing, in or outbound,
Give multiple exposures, environmentally found.

Humidity, temps, pressure, some high 'n some low,
Dramatically change, as pilot I know.
Its equally true, grocery shopping or show,
While fine when you enter, exits can be a blow!

The choices we make, as patients while ill,
Reflect how we feel, our fears and our skill.
We project strong desire, attitude and goodwill,
Protecting ourselves, we're involved by sheer will!

At last the time has come to assess whether my LVRS operation has been a success or not. I get to be the ultimate judge. My answers to my own questions are the evidence.

How do I feel? Can I breathe better? Play more? Do I have greater mobility? Greater function? How is my attitude? Am I my old self? Can I play golf? Has it impacted libido? How is my stamina? Strength? Endurance? Can I work? What are my limitations? Can I live on my own?

These and many more answers are essential for me.

Assessment Time

Eighteen months beyond, since operation's done,
Let's assess my results to see what I have won.
Breathing now is easier, but I still cannot run,
I'm told to "move near water; easier said than done!"

I still use all the meds I had, before that fateful day,
Have added seven new ones, to keep allergies at bay!
Lungs are much more sensitive, but I'm allowed to play,
As long as I am careful, I enjoy each holiday!

I'm able to attend events, I once was forced to pass,
Even languish in the sun, outside on the grass!
Meds are never far away; I carry them en-mass,
I'm always checking weather on, the other side of glass.

Big changes in the temp, still cause my lungs to crash,
Limits my activities to, each carefully chosen bash.
Tra-ve-ling is very harsh, may cost me lots of cash,
Especially in airports as, I dash from sash to sash!

Passing through security, I'm examined quite a spell,
Steel cable holding ster-num, rings the security bell!
Being stripped in glass cage, for Security Show 'n tell,
Makes my trips for poetry, something of a Hell!

I drive, live, love and laugh; do everything with glee,
Knowing life is limited, I'm happy to breathe free!
Doctors and caregivers, have bles-sed-ly helped me,
The Lord and my family have answered every plea!

There are many ways to share your love and thankfulness with others. Helping in the community, volunteering to do something of value for someone else: those and many more are examples or expression of thanks or good fortune. At one time or another, I have done all of them.

In this case, I choose to share the thankfulness for my good fortune in the form of a written word – poetry. To be honest, I had never written one line of poetry before this collection of words. Writing poetry has become the silver lining of my disease.

The goal of my writing is quite simply to help other COPD patients and their families. If readers of these words gain knowledge, understanding and insight into the COPD experience, then I will have done my job exactly the way I envisioned it.

I freely admit that I did not intend to write a book, only a few poems. However, once I shared those poems with my significant other, my medical teams, some friends and my family, all those people began encouraging me to write more. Once I became published and began to gain recognition for my writing, the die was cast.

Sharing My Love

Until you get ill, you never know the regret,
Of breathing freely or the joys that you'll get,
Doing simple daily chores; the fun we beget,
While walking in sun or singing in a quartet.

One moment you're fine, the next may be bad,
It's hard to predict the kind of day to be had.
For breathing is needed to do everything glad,
Sick lungs will forbid, you do anything rad'!

You drive down the road, smile on your face,
Suddenly you're coughing, as if hit with mace.
You impact your loved ones, those you embrace,
While one moment smiling, concern takes its place.

We count on our loved ones, to help us in need,
There's housing, loving and attentions to feed,
Yet caring for illness can force families to deed,
Lifetime possessions to those who praise greed!

I count my blessings, for in spite of my stew,
I'm joyfully sharing, prized possessions anew.
My poems tell stories; I share them with you,
'Tis my way of loving, before I bid you adieu.

Many of us choose to learn as much as we can about COPD, as well as share our knowledge with others. Each and every afflicted patient would jump at the chance to find and take a cure for this disease. Alternative medicines are always considered.

Many patients and loved ones gather on the COPD Chat Line at COPD-International.com to learn and share. (If you decide to join the chat line, just tell them, "Lee sent me!" They will know.)There are other chat lines as well. Other patients will take a more pro-active posture, going into the community trying to reach and teach the dangers of the disease and its causes. Still other patients (some of them medical professionals) do research and then share that knowledge with the rest of us for the benefit of all.

As my Resource Guide identifies, there are many efforts under way to help others. Patients and their loved ones are not alone. Most importantly for you to understand is this point – 'Most COPD patients will bend over backwards to help any other COPD patient, potential patient, caregiver or family member'.

Our Quest

COPD patients choose an e-ter-nal quest,
Seeking some answers to ward off this pest!
Exercise and diet are important to digest,
Help us keep fit, also breathing our best.

Medicine has given me all I dare ask,
Faith and my family supported that task.
I continue my search, before I can bask,
For better solutions, then I'll tap my cask!

I chat with my peers, on COPD chat,
Learn of experiences the others combat.
We share information and many a stat,
Have joys and sorrows; sometimes tip a hat.

Some of us take, the knowledge we gain,
Share it with others, to prevent further pain.
Teaching an audience a prevention refrain,
Trying to tap into, the smokers disdain!

So now we give back, to those new and old,
What knowledge we can, with nary a scold.
We're trying to help, the young, old and bold,
Prevent walking paths, of nightmares we've told.

Finally I have reached a point in my recovery where we can explore better medications. My Pulmonary doctor prescribed a new medication that is absolutely amazing to me! This new medication allows me to retire all of the old medications I once used. Instead of using four medications four times per day, now I only need to use two medications twice a day! What a blessing!

To put that into perspective, I used to spend 25 minutes, four times per day, medicating myself – a total of 100 minutes per day! Proper application of these medications dictates that you allow one minute between each puff of medicine and you must take two puffs of each medicine. Further, the best results are achieved if you allow five minutes between each different type of medicine. Once those applications are complete, it is important that you rinse your mouth to clear medication build-up and prevent further complications. The process is very time consuming and interferes with just about everything you want to do in life.

Here is one more very important point. While my old medications were steroid based, my new medications do not include any steroids - another huge blessing! It is like being released from a 'jail' of sorts – breathing more freely, deeper, feeling better, having more energy, being more alert, having more time to do things with less interference, able to participate in life again – life is great!

They tell me that even better medications are in the pipeline! Hooray! I can hardly wait!

Finally!

My breathing became better, now it's mostly back,
This newest med they gave me, really has the knack!
Now I can breathe deeper, with half the dose per whack,
Super strong inhalers, retired the whole stack!

I'm using half the meds I did scant days ago,
Sleeping hours are longer, now candles I can blow!
My spirits are on high; the energy does flow,
Now I must be careful, to tell myself to "Whoa!"

Five days ago I took naps, some-times two a day,
Now I do not need them, there's energy to play!
Eagerly I sing a song, tap my foot – olay?
Would someone point me to a dragon I can slay?!

Swinging golf clubs to and fro, sons will be surprised,
Gonna be real careful, to keep myself disguised!
Sons have waited for five years, even have chastised,
Hoping I'd recover, so my golf is reprised!

I still need some oxygen, only ten percent,
Needing fewer meds now, means time is better spent!
Sleeping, eating, playing, each act is Heaven sent,
Giving me more freedom, returning me to gent!

What a thrill this day is, my burden is in flight,
Breathing free means spirits soar, right out of my sight!
Happy, humming, humorous, my life is delight,
At long last my future, is once again real bright!

I consider myself to be blessed. While I have this terrible affliction called COPD, I've been lucky enough to have had and survived my LVRS operation. Very few are so lucky! I am satisfied with the results because I can breathe so much easier. I've had Pulmonary Rehabilitation, some good days and bad, so now I must go forward to see what lies ahead. Isn't the human spirit a marvel?

Getting On With Life

I've had an operation, that lets me breathe new life,
Into lungs made smaller by, the wielding of a knife.
Doctors take good care of me, as if it's only rife,
Now I make the most of things, avoiding any strife.

At sixty-six I enjoy life, in spite of my disease,
My operation gave me time to do just what I please.
Each moment is a precious gift I waste not in the breeze,
Now I'm on a mission of, loving while I tease!

Things I love are fam-i-ly, the music I adore,
Fragrant flowers all around, a placid lakeside shore.
Dawn brings hope and visuals, reaching to my core,
And a loving lady who, pleases me galore!

Grandkids make my heart swell, just calling me by name,
Give my spirit wings to fly, while playing childish game.
I share with all my children, by loving each the same,
And always say "I love you", it is this father's claim.

If I meet an ailing friend who needs some help I say,
"Is there something I can do to ease your path today?"
To others I encounter, along this wondrous way,
Teasing grins, loving smiles, witticisms for the day.

My path is set, vision clear, I know what I must do,
Living, loving, laughing, helping when it's due.
The years I've left are cherished, all my memories too,
I'm bound to blaze one more trail, before I bid adieu.

Before we pass from life on Earth, I think we all should write a letter to our dad, or to our mom if that is more appropriate for you. My father died at the tender age of 38 years due to extreme complications of diabetes. He had little or no chance to see the development of those he sired and never achieved his own full potential.

As his 'surprise child' and the eldest of his four sons, I enjoyed having him around and learning from him for almost thirteen years. I embody many of his attributes, have implemented most of his teachings, gotten into trouble much the way he did as a boy and used the things he and mom taught me as a foundation on which to build my life.

As a self-made man, I like to think that I have developed myself into someone who has achieved much, conducted myself well and developed into the kind of person my father would have been proud to call – son. Here is my way of telling him so.

Letter To Dad

Starting as farm boy, I loved family, work, life,
With animals, land, orchards, amid medical strife.
You died young, leaving four boys and your wife,
Suddenly homeless, penniless, not even a fife!

The lessons you taught became invaluable then,
Persevere, be resourceful, me two years past ten.
Use ethics and pride with all labors 'round den,
Do the best that you can, many doors will o-pen.

Give back to community. Help those that you can.
Be honest and forthright, to become a good man.
Use compassion with others, whether student or clan,
And with your strong wit, be bold with your plan!

We struggled five years, 'til I joined the Marines,
Fulfilling my vow, by wearing the greens.
Moved into computers to work with machines,
Created Control Programs, fulfilled many dreams.

I learned something new, every day of my life,
Gave you four grandkids, they're sharp as a knife!
Did the best that I could with work, family and wife,
Sent you my brother; caused Mom lots of strife!

I helped with the deaf and homebound you see,
Sang songs for the aged, afflicted and thee,
Gave money, food, clothes, to help the need-y,
Hope you've been watching, proud as can be!

I followed your footsteps, some good 'n some bad,
Behaved like a gentleman, was never called cad.
Thanks for your name, 'twas the best that you had,
Hope I've done honor, for Gordon, my dad.

It is my fervent hope that you have gained insight into living with this disease called COPD. While I have written about my form of this dread disease, there are many other forms. I have tried to provide the basic knowledge every COPD patient and related family member needs to know. In all honesty, I have only scratched the surface.

I suggest that you review the Glossary of Terms and the Resource Guide on the following pages. Updated information for the Resource Guide can be found on my web site: **www.my-oh-my.com**.

I have taken the time to digitally record each of my poems. If you would like to purchase a copy, drop me a note and we will make arrangements for you to get a copy for yourself. Please be advised that I am not a recording artist either! That CD information will also be found on my website once it is ready.

I welcome your feedback at: Huffin-n-puffin@bigfoot.com

In closing, allow me to quote a wall plaque hanging beside my back door. I see and read it every time I leave the house. Listed as an 'unknown author', here is the inscription:

"Who we are is God's gift to us.
What we become is our gift to God."

Author Unknown

I hope your spirit rises to meet the challenges you encounter. Breathe easy.

Leland Gordon Vogel

GLOSSARY of fairly common COPD terms/names:

This Glossary presents a few of the terms and medication names encountered as we experience COPD. This glossary does not begin to address all of the terms or medicines that might be applied to a COPD condition. In the Resources Guide, I have provided a link to a COPD Glossary that offers a more thorough definition and description. Just as there are many variations of cancer, COPD is equally complex and unique to each individual.

I am not a medical professional nor would I begin to presume to know it all. However, these terms are enough to help get someone oriented, basically knowledgeable and headed in the right direction. I strongly recommend that people learn as much as possible about their particular form of the disease. There is an ever-increasing wealth of information available on the Internet.

Albuterol® – a prescribed short-term lung relief inhaler

Atrovent® - a prescribed COPD inhaler medication

Aerobics – exercises that build stamina, increase heart rate

Azmacort® – a prescribed inhaler for asthma, more

BiPAP® – a machine that administers pressurized air via a Facemask

Blood Test – removal of blood samples for a variety of tests, done repeatedly

Blood Gas Test – special form of blood test to measure oxygen in the blood

Bronchitis – an inflammation of the bronchial airways

Cannula – the headpiece of plastic tubing that delivers oxygen into the nose of the user

Cat Scan – a process of taking several x-rays as you lay on a sliding table

Caregiver/s – anyone who helps your COPD needs; family, loved ones, professionals

COPD – Chronic Obstructive Pulmonary Disorder, has many origins

CPAP® – a test for oxygenation of the blood

Diagnosis – the process of identifying an ailment

Edema – retention of fluids (water) in the body

EKG - Electrocardiogram – monitors, measures and reports heart activity

Emphysema – a disease that destroys lung tissue, elasticity and traps air in the lung

Endurance – length of time you can move before requiring support

Echocardiogram – a test to examine heart activity via ultrasound and record the results on videotape

Facemask – protective paper, cloth or plastic mask/s worn over the mouth and nose

Flovent® – a prescribed inhaler medication

ICU – Intensive Care Unit, a carefully supervised/monitored hospital room

Incision – a cut on the body made by a surgeon for surgery

Inhaler/s – one of a number of medicine 'puffers' inhaled by mouth to aid breathing

Lungs – sacks (think dense sponges) of tissue that capture, process and release air for the body

LVRS – Lung Volume Reduction Surgery – an operation to remove diseased lung tissue

Mobility – the act of moving your body around from place to place to do necessary things/chores

Nebulizer® – a method of delivering inhaled medicine/s into the lungs

Nuclear Medicine – X-ray facilities

Nurse Practitioner – a person with GP skills who lacks full credentials

Oximeter® - a device 'clipped' onto the finger to measure blood oxygenation

Oxygen, Compressor – adjustable machine that compresses room oxygen for consumption

Oxygen, Liquid – oxygen delivered in 20 or 30-gallon tanks for human consumption

Oxygen, Portable – 5-pound portable tanks of liquid oxygen taken from larger tanks

Oxygen Carrier – a wheeled carrier for portable oxygen tanks, often with expanding handle

Oxygenation – the measurable amount of air carried through your body in/by your blood

PFT - Pulmonary Function Test – measures the volume of air your lungs exchange

Pharmacist – a doctor of medicine who dispenses, verifies and teaches medications

Phlegm/Sputum – the thick fluid gunk patients cough from their chest

Plastic Hose - the 4-50 foot 'umbilical cord' between patient and their oxygen tank/s

Pulmonologist – a physician who specializes in lung/chest diseases

Quinine – one medicine used to prevent muscle cramping

Red Heart Pillow – a red, heart shaped pillow donated to chest surgery patients

Serevent® – a prescribed medication for COPD

Spacer – a large plastic tube placed between inhaler and mouth; maximizes medication application

Spirogram – a Spirometry report showing lung volumes

Spirometer® – a device that measures inhaled/exhaled oxygen volumes from the lungs

Spiriva® - a new 'super medication' – a single application/day

Stamina – durable strength of organ and body functions while moving

Steel Cable – woven steel wire used to tie sternum together after open chest operations

Steroids – some inhaler medications use steroids as an active ingredient

Sternum – the front bone down the middle of your chest holding ribs together

Stress – anything causing increase in blood pressure, anxiety, stimulation

Pulmonary Rehab – physical exercises that are supervised and/or monitored by a therapist

Therapist – supervisor/coach of pulmonary rehab regimens

Thoracic Surgeon – a physician who specializes in heart/lung surgeries

Treadmill – an electrically powered walking device used for walking and jogging exercises

Weights – hand/leg/arm weights (3+ lbs) used to strengthen body during rehab

NOTE:

Albuterol, Atrovent, Azmacort, Flovent, Foradil, Oximeter, Serevent, Spirometer, Spiriva, BiPAP and CPAP are registered trademarks of these companies: GlaxoSmithKline, Dura Pharmaceuticals, Inc., Boehringer Ingelheim International GMBH Corp., Glaxo Group Ltd., Rorer Pharmaceutical Corp., Ciba-Geigy Corp., Flomericas Ltd., Respironics, Inc., Nellcor Inc., Union Carbide, Hudson Respiratory Care Inc.

COPD Resource Guide

This Guide offers you the opportunity to learn about and under-stand COPD in all of its manifestations. You can also learn about LVRS and other treatment forms available for the disease. This guide focuses on access to the Internet because it is fast, free and readily available to the masses.

American Lung Association: www.lungusa.org

COPD International Website: www.copd-international.com

COPD Newsletter, Help Line, Smoking Cessation link, more

COPD Chat Line: www.copd-international.com/mainchat.htm
COPD patients chat, exchange ideas and info, help
new patients.

COPD Disease Glossary:
www.members.tripod.com/noairtogo/gloss.htm#glossary
COPD Terms and Definitions

Stop Smoking For Teens:
www.geocities.com/HotSprings/Spa/7154/index.html
*** See Ron Peterson's Straw Mask creation ***
www.preventionvideo.org

Portable Oxygen: A User's Perspective (by Pete Wilson)
www.portableoxygen.org

Spiriva (spy-re-va) - Newest COPD medication:
www.drugsnewsnetwork.com/news/spiriva-approved.html

Living With COPD (by Bill Powell Corporation/Foundation)
www.papapoo.com
www.copd-support.com

AARC - American Association of Respiratory Care
www.aarc.org

Mt. Sinai Hospital – Pulmonary Care Center
www.mtsinai.org/pulmonary/index.html

NEF - National Emphysema Foundation
www.emphysemafoundation.org

Cheshire Medical Center:
www.cheshire-med.com/programs/pulrehab/rehinfo.html
See patient Bill Horden's materials

Pulmonary Research and Education Foundation
www.perf2ndwind.org/index.html
Look for LVRS, Breaking News, 2nd Wind Newsletter

COPD Related illnesses and Support: www.supportpath.com

COPD Dietary Cooking: www.thekitchenlink.com/search3.html

COPD Digest – a periodical for professionals and patients
www.copd-digest.org

Drugs and Pharmaceuticals (COPD and others)
www.rxlist.com
Site includes **16-minute web-cast** info about LVRS,
medication conflicts, more

Health & Human Services – WebMD connection:
www.hhs.webmd.com

Getting your Insurance Company to pay:
www.thyroid.about.com/cs/newsresearch/a/insurancepay

Military Healthcare Services
Veterans Administration: www.va.gov
Dept. of Defense: www.tricare.osd.mil

The Breathing Space – Inhalers, Medications, Nebulizers
www.combivent.com/index.htm

Medicare and COPD: www.medicare.gov/health/copd.asp

Allergy Information:
www.healthscout.com/news/1/518539/main.html

Travel with Oxygen:
www.ruralnorthwest.com/artman/publish/article_3856

Cruise Lines Travel with Oxygen:
www.medicaltravel.org/oxygen/24hour.html

Prescription Drugs via Canada:
www.medicationscanada.com
www.pillscanada.com/
www.pillscanada.com/seniors/indez.php
www.prescripnet.com/index.asp

NEW MEDICAL PROCEDURES FOR COPD
Lung Valve (LVRS without the big operation):
www.emphasysmedical.com

NEWEST THERAPY EXERCISES
Learn Harmonica: www.harmonicacountry.com

Alternative Medications, Treatment & Procedures
Live Cell Therapy: www.livecelltherapy.org

COPD Advocacy Groups
American Lung Assoc. www.lungusa.org
EFFORTS http://www.emphysema.net
CPOD-Alert www.copd-alert.com